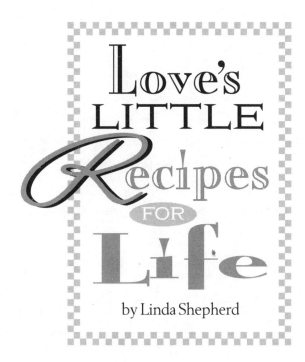

Love's
LITTLE
Recipes
FOR
Life

by Linda Shepherd

MULTNOMAH BOOKS SISTERS, OREGON

LOVE'S LITTLE RECIPES FOR LIFE
published by Multnomah Books
a part of the Questar publishing family

© 1997 by Linda E. Shepherd

International Standard Book Number: 1-57673-094-8

Cover Design by Susan Luckey Higdon

Printed in the United States of America

Most Scripture quotations are from the *New International Version*
© 1973, 1984 by International Bible Society,
used by permission of Zondervan Publishing House
Also quoted:
The King James Version (KJV)
The New King James Version (NKJV)
© 1984 by Thomas Nelson, Inc.

For information:
QUESTAR PUBLISHERS, INC.
POST OFFICE BOX 1720
SISTERS, OREGON 97759
Library of Congress Cataloging-in-Publication Data:
Shepherd, Linda E., 1957–
Love's little recipes for life/by Linda Shepherd.
p.cm.
ISBN 1-57673-094-8
1. Cookery. II. Title.
TX714.S53 1997
242—dc21   96-52185
                                                                     CIP
97 98 99 00 01 02 03 04 05 06 — 10 9 8 7 6 5 4 3 2 1

*T*able of Contents

When it comes to food for thought,

feast, don't diet.

L.E.S.

To my mom and dad—who always
set a feast of love and
wisdom in our home.

*I*ntroduction

Every cook knows that flour, yeast, oil, sugar and water do not make bread unless care is taken to sift, stir, knead, allow to rise and to bake the dough at the proper temperature. This book is designed to show you how to blend the detailed ingredients of your life.

Not only will *Love's Little Recipes* guide you to select and mix choice fixin's, it will show you what you knead after you measure your love, sift your thoughts and rise above your circumstances. You'll learn to select the proper speed as you beat the odds for happiness.

As you start cooking, you'll enjoy not only tasty results but the fun of preparing your dishes for the wonderful buffet called life.

Linda E. Shepherd

~ NOTICE ~

From St. Paul's Methodist Episcopal Church Cookbook, Cedar Rapids, Iowa, 1915

Listen to our tale of woe and triumph.

We, the friends of the cook, known by the general name RECIPE,
do hereby affirm that we are trusted by the persons who claim to have tried us
and found us not wanting. What agony we have suffered in our many trials—
at the hands of inexperienced persons who did not adhere
to our directions—not but ourselves know!

The fact that we have been esteemed worthy to shine in this
book proves our triumph.

Some of us originally belonged to others, but owing to our good qualities
we became friends to many. Thus, we present ourselves to you,
trusting you will try us and prove us friends to all.

Part One

ે▲

Gathering Life's Basic Ingredients

The first duty of love is to listen.

Paul Tillich

Chapter One

❧

Spoonfuls of Love

There is no instinct like that of the heart.

Lord Byron

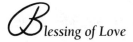

Blessing of Love

Lord, you've made me rich with love so I can spend it on others.
Let my love simmer; may it never burn those to whom I serve it.
Help me spread love to family and friends so they will not only
believe in themselves, but believe in you. Amen.

L.E.S

Love comforteth like sunshine after rain.

William Shakespeare

ℬe My Valentine Cookie

Cook's Note: *This is an anytime gift from the heart you can give to someone special, including yourself!*

Ingredients:

1 cup butter, at room temperature
1 1/2 cups confectioner's sugar
1 egg
1/2 teaspoon lemon extract

2 1/2 cups flour
1 teaspoon soda
1 teaspoon cream of tartar

Directions:

Cream butter with confectioner's sugar. Add egg and extract. Blend in flour, soda and cream of tartar. Cover and chill 2 hours. Heat oven to 375°. On floured surface, roll dough into thin layer, 1/8-inch thick. Cut into valentines with cookie cutter and place on lightly greased baking sheet. Bake until very light brown, 7 or 8 minutes.

Icing:

1 cup confectioner's sugar
1 1/2 tablespoons milk
1 teaspoon vanilla

Few drops of red food coloring
Decorative sprinkles

Directions:

Mix ingredients until smooth.
When cookies are cool, spread with icing and sprinkles.

*L*ove's Little Shopping List

Lettuce be kind to one another.

Ketchup on old friendships.

Soup up your day with smiles.

Turnip your nose at holding grudges.

Leek joy to others.

Beet the blues.

Chips in and do your part.

Pepper your loved ones with kisses.

Salt your life with good deeds.

Orange you glad you're alive?
Thank God!

Pear your heart with others.

Pop in and see a friend.

Jam your mind with good books.

Spread your day with God's word.

Dial your spouse to say, "I love you!"

Shout out a greeting to a friend.

Whisk off and complete a project
you started.

Bold yourself. Try something new.

Tidy up your home.

Huggies for everyone.

Pampers yourself with a nap.

Fresh Start for mistakes.

New Era for positive changes.

Glad for a new day.

L.E.S.

Chapter Two

ð

Dashes of Happiness

Happiness is made to be shared.

Folk Proverb

*R*ecipe *for a Well-Done Day*

Splash your face with water cold,
Feel the morning air.
Watch the sunrise edged with gold,
Breath a humble prayer.

Serve a warm and friendly smile,
Add a pinch of humor.
See a friend and talk awhile,
Never start a rumor.

Give your heart to those you love,
Work hard for all your pay;
Turn your thoughts to God above,
To make a well-done day.

L.E.S.

His master replied, "Well done, good and faithful servant!"

Matthew 25:23

*R*ecipe *for a Happy Home*

Ingredients:
1 husband
1 wife
Handful of children
Generous portions of prayer
3 cups love, firmly packed
1 package work
1 package play
1 portion patience
1 portion discipline
1 can kisses
Pinch of salt

Directions:

Mix all ingredients thoroughly and sprinkle with the salt of awareness. Bake daily in a moderate oven fueled by the forgiveness of old grudges and past unpleasantness. Cool home and turn out onto a platter garnished with cheerfulness and laughter. Serve in large helpings.

Serves God, country and community.

Author Unknown, *Butter 'n Love Recipes*

It Couldn't be Done

Somebody said that it couldn't be done,
But he with a chuckle replied
That "maybe it couldn't," but he would be one
Who wouldn't say so 'til he'd tried.

So he buckled right in with the trace of a grin
On his face. If he worried he hid it.
He started to sing as he tackled the thing
That couldn't be done and he did it.

Edgar A. Guest

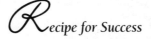

ecipe for Success

Cook's Note: *Combined with ambition, these ingredients can produce as much success as needed.*

Ingredients:
1/4 cup cooperation
1 ounce common sense
2 cups honesty
4 cups perseverance
5 tablespoons enthusiasm
1 quart hard work marinated in prayer

Directions:
Call upon your good character to help you blend these ingredients. Bake until golden opportunities arise. Spread warm success with courtesy. Enjoy.

L.E.S.

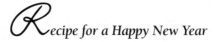

ecipe for a Happy New Year

Ingredients:
12 fresh months
20 gallons forgiveness
5 pounds hope
4 quarts resolutions
1 Bible
365 dates
Constant prayer

Directions:
Mix months, forgiveness and hope with resolutions of your choice. As you continuously stir, read Bible for guidance. Add dates one by one. Mix with constant prayer. Sprinkle your new year with grins. This dish is not meant to be consumed alone: share generously with friends and family.

L.E.S.

Chapter Three

ða

Cupfuls of Knowing God

"It is written:

'Man does not live on bread alone,

but on every word that comes from the mouth of God.'"

Matthew 4:4

Ten Little Recipes for Finding God's Will

It seems as if everyone is searching to find God's will. I've chosen my ten favorite recipes for finding God's will from my favorite cookbook, The Good Book. Some of these dishes may seem hard to swallow, but they are nutritious and nourishing with a sweet after-taste. If you follow these recipes, you will never have heart-burn.

L.E.S.

1. Live Your Life with Love

Jesus replied: "'Love the Lord your God with all your heart and with all your soul and with all your mind.' This is the first and greatest commandment. And the second is like it: 'Love your neighbor as yourself.'"

Matthew 22:37-39

2. Forgive Everyone

"Bear with each other and forgive whatever grievances you may have against one another. Forgive as the Lord forgave you."

Colossians 3:13

3. Seek God

"Ask and it will be given to you; seek and you will find; knock and the door will be opened to you. For everyone who asks receives; he who seeks finds; and to him who knocks, the door will be opened."

Matthew 7:7-8

4. Believe

"For God so loved the world that he gave his one and only Son, that whoever believes in him shall not perish but have eternal life."

John 3:16

5. Rejoice in the Lord Always

"Be joyful always; pray continually; give thanks in all circumstances, for this is God's will for you in Christ Jesus."

1 Thessalonians 5:16-18

6. Trust

"Do not let your hearts be troubled. Trust in God; trust also in me."

John 14:1

7. Repent from Your Sins

Jesus began to preach, "Repent, for the kingdom of heaven is near."

Matthew 4:17

8. Share Your Faith

"I pray that you may be active in sharing your faith, so that you will have a full understanding of every good thing we have in Christ."

Philemon 1:6

9. Fill Your Life with Prayer

"The end of all things is near. Therefore be clear minded and self-controlled so that you can pray."

1 Peter 4:7

10. Study God's Word

"Study to show thyself approved unto God, a workman that needeth not to be ashamed, rightly dividing the word of truth."

2 Timothy 2:15 (KJV)

O'Day's Prayer

There once was a girl named O'Day
Who prayed by yakking away.
She chattered all night,
From dusk until light
And missed all that God had to say.

Prayer For Life

Praise His name.
Request forgiveness and help.
Acquit those who wrong you.
Yearn to listen for His voice.
Expect God to answer.
Remember the needs of others.

L.E.S.

*S*cripture Cake

Cook's Note: *This is a real cake that will help you know God. Tell your friends and family you got it right out of the Bible. It's worth the extra effort to look up all the verses. For best result use the New International Version.*

Ingredients:
Cake
2 cups Genesis 18:6 (flour)

1 1/2 cups Jeremiah 6:20 (sugar)

3 1/2 teaspoons Matthew 13:33 (baking powder)

1 teaspoon Leviticus 2:13 (salt)

1/2 cup Proverbs 30:33 (softened butter)

1 cup Judges 5:25 (milk)

1 teaspoon 1 Chronicles 9:30 (vanilla)

3 Isaiah 10:14 (eggs)

Filling
Stir together the following:

3/4 cup Job 20:17 (frosting)

1/2 cup Song of Solomon 6:11 (coconut)

1/4 cup Numbers 17:8 (almonds)

1/2 cup Genesis 1:12 (cherries)

Frosting

1/2 cup Proverbs 30:33 (melt butter in saucepan)
1 cup Jeremiah 6:20 (stir in brown sugar and heat to a boil)
Exodus 16:23 (keep at boil and stir constantly for 2 minutes)
1/2 cup Judges 5:25 (stir in milk)
Exodus 16:23 (heat to boiling)
Jeremiah 18:14 (cool for five minutes)
2 cups Proverbs 24:14 (stir in sweet confectioner's sugar)
Matthew 7:27 (beat until fluffy)

Directions:

1. Genesis 31:40 (heat oven to 350°)
2. Deuteronomy 27:2 (coat 2 round 9 inch pans with grease and flour)
3. Malachi 3:10 (pour cake ingredients into mixing bowl)
4. Proverbs 23:14 (beat at medium speed until mixed)
5. Genesis 18:16 (bake 40-45 minutes)
6. Jeremiah 18:14 (cool)
7. Proverbs 30:33 (churn ingredients for frosting)
8. Genesis 43:11 (make filling)
9. Exodus 29:2 (spread filling between layers of cake and on top)
10. Exodus 16:23 (add 3 tablespoons boiling water to remaining frosting)
11. Acts 12:24 (spread frosting on cake)

Part Two

&

How to Use Life's Seasonings

"'I was a stranger and you invited me in.'"

Matthew 25:35

Chapter Four

Pepper with Hellos

A smile is the shortest distance between two people.

Anonymous

How to End Loneliness

If you're wearing dark blinders
Here's a reminder
To stop and unmask your eyes.
If lonely you're feeling
Have you tried appealing
To others you often pass by?
Stop and reach out to
Others who need you.
And friends will be in supply.
For those who are friendly
Find it no mystery.
With others they oft unify.

L.E.S.

*The door of the human heart can only be
opened from the inside and love is the key.*

L.E.S.

Make a Friend

Cook's Note: *To make a friend you must first be a friend.*

Ingredients:
1 good sense of humor
1 dozen smiles
2 quarts helpfulness
1 pint consideration
3 cups conversation
5 tablespoons questions
At least one invitation

Directions:

To be a friend, select an acquaintance you think will agree with your sense of humor. Offer smiles, helpfulness, consideration and conversation. Ask basic questions about her interests, work and hobbies. Invite your acquaintance for a walk, chat, tea or dinner. Exchange phone numbers, tips and recipes. The next thing you know your acquaintance is your friend.

If you see your efforts are not establishing a connection, keep trying or repeat the process with another acquaintance.

L.E.S.

I Shall Not Pass This Way Again

Through this toilsome world, alas!
Once and only once I pass;
If a kindness I may show,
If a good deed I may do
For a suffering fellow man,
Let me do it while I can.
No delay, for it is plain
I shall not pass this way again.

Unknown

*A good listener is not only popular everywhere,
but after a while he knows something.*
Wilson Mizner, American Humorist

*R*ecipe to Greet a New Neighbor

Cook's Note: *This is a great recipe to use when you see a moving van unload in your neighborhood.*

Ingredients:
4 tablespoons boldness
Half-a-dozen smiles
1 or more open doors
1 pleasant greeting
1 well-baked introduction

Directions:

Do not observe new neighbors from behind closed curtains. Select a heaping of boldness and mix with a smile. Open your door and walk across the street or next door. Give your new neighbor a pleasant greeting: "Welcome to the neighborhood," followed by an introduction.

You may wish to add an invitation such as, "Would you like to come over for coffee and Good Neighbor Coffee Cake?" (recipe follows).

L.E.S.

Good Neighbor Coffee Cake

Ingredients/Batter
1 cup butter
1 cup sugar
3 eggs
1 teaspoon vanilla
1 cup sour cream
2 teaspoons soda
1 teaspoon baking powder
2 cups flour

Filling
1/2 cup ground nuts
3/4 cup (packed) brown sugar
2 tablespoons flour
2 tablespoons butter
1 tablespoon cinnamon

Topping
Powdered sugar for dusting top

Directions:

Cream butter, then slowly add sugar. Beat well. Stir in eggs. Add vanilla and sour cream, blending well. In separate bowl mix flour, baking powder and soda. Slowly add to egg mixture.

In separate bowl, mix filling ingredients with a fork until crumbly.

Pour half of the batter into greased angel food cake pan. Place a layer of crumbs over the batter. Pour the remaining batter over layer of crumbs. Bake at 350° for about 1 hour. Serve with coffee and a neighborly chat.

L.E.S.

Chapter Five

۶**

Savory Good-Byes

Parting is such sweet sorrow....

William Shakespeare, *Romeo and Juliet*

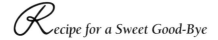

Recipe for a Sweet Good-Bye

Ingredients:
Tea in china teacups for two
Something sweet
1 pint of loving words
1 gallon of recalled memories
2 handkerchiefs, suitable for wiping tears
1 notepad and pen
1 dozen prestamped and addressed stationery tied in a bow
Warm hugs (as many as you wish to serve)
1 moving blessing

Directions:
Many people avoid this dish but sometimes circumstances make serving it necessary. To serve: invite your friend over for tea. Pass out memories to share. Exchange loving words and do not be embarrassed if salty tears result. Distribute handkerchiefs and use as needed. Use your notepad and pen to write down your friend's new phone number and address. Present her with bundle of stationery pre-addressed to you.

When it is time to part, share as many hugs as necessary and give your friend a blessing for moving.

L.E.S.

Moving Away Blessing

Dear God,

Please bless my dear friend as she starts a journey
to a new home in a new place. Go with her and let her feel your care.
Keep our hearts united and help us stay in touch through our prayers, calls and letters.
Thank you for allowing me the privilege to be a part of her life. Amen.

L.E.S.

*H*ow to Leave a Friend

Cook's Note: *If you must move away from your dear friend, don't go without leaving something behind.*

Ingredients:

1 portion of your heart
2 cups leftover laughter

1 quart memory preserves
1 forwarding address and phone number

Directions:

When you leave a friend behind, be sure to leave a portion of your heart with her. Add leftover laughter and preserved memories. Give her your forwarding address and phone number. Once you are gone, be sure to write and call, stirring memories and laughter for as long as you stay connected.

Forever Friend

Distance can never part
The ties that bind our hearts.
For though we've said good-byes
And though great distance lies

To separate our ways
Your presence with me stays.
For love I'll always send
To you, my forever friend.

L.E.S.

A friend loves at all times.
Proverbs 17:17

College-Bound Blessing

I have held you close. Now as you fly into adulthood, bound to open books and discover new worlds, I release you. But not without one final prayer—prosper not only in your studies, but prosper in knowing God more richly.

I will not be there to catch you when you fall. But God will catch you when I can't. Depend on Him and learn to trust Him. You are not alone. Knowing this, my empty nest will not seem so lonely. My heart will soar as I watch you take wing.

L.E.S.

Chapter Six

ૐ

Thyme of Sorrow

Heavy hearts, like heavy clouds in the sky,
are best relieved by the letting of water.

Antoine Rivarol, French Critic

Recipe for a Good Cry

Cook's Note: *Do not hold your tears back in this recipe.*
The more you use, the better the results.

Ingredients:
Gush of tears
Box of tissues
5 or more minutes of solitude

Directions:

We sometimes keep our feelings bottled inside. But in ancient times, women released them in order to capture tears in tiny keepsake bottles. Feelings must be released through tears so that pressure will escape our emotional cooker.

For a good cry, go to your bedroom with a box of tissues. Close the door and allow feelings to surface until they overflow, 5 to 30 minutes (or longer) each time. If you are experiencing severe pressure, you may need to repeat this process for several days. This will help prevent emotional explosions and deep depressions.

L.E.S.

There is a time for everything, and a season for every activity under heaven:
...a time to weep and a time to laugh, a time to mourn and a time to dance.

Ecclesiastes 3:1,4

When Sorrow Knocks

When Sorrow knocked upon my door
I tried to bid her leave.
Instead she sat upon my floor
And there began to weave.

She wove a woe so deep and wide
From streams of anguished tears.
I tried to cast her grief aside;
It tangled in my fears.

Now Sorrow's gone, I'm glad to say
My grief is much relieved.
But, oh, so much I learned the day
That she began to weave.

L.E.S.

Where, O death, is your victory? Where, O death, is your sting?

1 Corinthians 15:55

Death is merely a comma in the journey of life.

Anonymous

*Do not be anxious about anything, but in everything, by prayer and petition,
with thanksgiving, present your requests to God.*

Philippians 4:6

Recipe to Flavor Sorrow with Joy

Cook's Note: *The secret of joy is this: it is not only found despite sorrow, it may be found because of sorrow.*

Ingredients:
2 cups sorrow
1 cup thanks
All circumstances
1 part bitterness
Unlimited time

Directions:
Blend sorrow and thanks with circumstances. This will yield new perspectives.

Let go of bitterness, dropping into pot gently, remembering Psalm 30:5—*Weeping may remain for a night, but rejoicing comes in the morning.*

Simmer ingredients, adding time minute by minute. Do not undercook. Your sorrows will be fully flavored with joy.

L.E.S.

Chapter Seven

Salt with Joy

Optimism: A cheerful frame of mind that enables a tea kettle to sing,
though in hot water up to its neck.

Anonymous

Preserving Memories

Every new day brings with it 86,000 fresh seconds. These seconds must be used before midnight to prevent spoilage. Today's time cannot be saved for tomorrow as today's time never keeps. You cannot use yesterday's time today as yesterday's time has already been consumed. You may not gather tomorrow's time today as tomorrow's time is not ripe.

Moments used today can be preserved as flavorful memories. They will bring smiles to the many tomorrows to come.

L.E.S.

Keep your face to the sunshine and you cannot see the shadow.

Helen Keller, American Writer

Never buy blessings on sale—they should be counted, not discounted.

L.E.S.

If you forget the language of gratitude,
you can never be on speaking terms with happiness.

L.E.S.

Happiness consists of living each day as if it were the
first day of your honeymoon and the last day of your vacation.

Anonymous

Whip Up a Good Attitude

Cook's Note: *You must create a good attitude yourself. It cannot be purchased in a store.*
A good attitude is like apple pie: when shared with others,
it's a picnic; kept to oneself, it might spoil.

Ingredients:
16 ounces cooperation
5 pounds forgiveness
1 bushel praise
1 smile
1 listening ear
Pint of calm spirit

Directions:
Blend all ingredients in a vessel of prayer. As you stir, you may notice the residue of heartache, sorrow and hard times rising to the top. Do not skim. You will find that these impurities enhance good attitude with the delicate flavor of love and patience. Good attitude may be hard to digest when you are tired or cranky. A nap or coffee break may aid digestion and allow you to keep a good attitude all day. In event of a tense situation, a serving of good attitude will be enjoyed by all. Keep plenty on hand, ready for any occasion.

L.E.S.

Apple Pie with an Open Face

Cook's Note: *Everyone knows that apple pies stimulate smiles. Add this dish to your table and watch the faces of your family and friends brighten.*

Ingredients:
4 1/2 cups sliced, pared apples
1 unbaked 9-inch pie shell
1 cup brown sugar
3 tablespoon flour
Pinch of salt
1/3 cup light cream
1/2 teaspoon cinnamon

Directions:
Combine sugar, flour and salt. Add cream. Stir until well blended. Pour cream mixture over apples and arrange apples in pie shell. Sprinkle with cinnamon. Cover the pie with aluminum foil. Bake at 375° for one hour. Remove foil and bake for an additional 30 minutes or until apples are tender. Serve with good attitude.

The best thing to put into a homemade pie is your teeth.

Anonymous

Part Three

?

Side-by-Side Dishes

Two are better than one, because they have a good return for their work.

Ecclesiastes 4:10

Chapter Eight

ह

Friendship Mix

Friendship is the greatest of worldly goods.

C. S. Lewis, British Author and Theologian

Friendship Cake to Sweeten Life

Step 1: Sourdough Starter.
Combine in large glass or ceramic bowl:
>   3 cups flour
>   1 cup sugar
>   1 package active dry yeast

Step 2: Gradually add 2 cups of warm milk
>   (between 105° and 115°). Cover with a cloth
>   and let stand in warm place for three days. Stir once a day.

Step 3: To make cake, combine the following ingredients:
>   2 teaspoons baking power
>   2 teaspoons soda
>   3 eggs
>   2 teaspoons vanilla
>   1/2 teaspoon salt
>   1 cup sugar
>   2 teaspoons cinnamon
>   1/3 cup oil
>   1 cup flour
>   1 cup sourdough starter

Fold in a total of one cup, singly or in any combination:
    Ripe banana
    Pineapple, drained
    Raisins
    Coconut
    Fruit cocktail, drained
    Chopped nuts
    Pour into greased and floured 9" X 11" or bunt cake pan.
    Bake at 350° for 45 to 60 minutes, or until done. Take one
    friendship cake, a copy of the written recipe on a card,
    and one cup of starter to a friend.

Step 4:

To replenish starter after use, add:
    1 cup milk (luke warm)
    1 cup flour
    1/2 cup sugar
    Stir until smooth. Let stand in warm place, at least 8 hours,
    until the mixture bubbles. Refrigerate, loosely covered. Use
    and replenish at least once every two weeks.

A Recipe for Friendship

Ingredients:
Two pair of feet
Two sets of walking shoes

Directions:

Two pair of feet in walking shoes meet, without sidestepping one another. Turn in the same direction.

If one foot should step on the other's toes, an apology is due. If the other's toes should be stepped upon, forgiveness is called for.

Two pair of feet walk, side-by-side, as long as the road may lead.

Adapted from unknown source, L.E.S.

Friendship Blessing

Lord, bless my friend and allow us to plant groves of happy memories.
May we always till the ground of our friendship with the nutrients of consideration, patience,
and care. Help our friendship to produce the fruit of love, honesty, and forgiveness.

L.E.S.

Greater love hath no man than this, that a man lay down his life for his friends.

John 15:13 (KJV)

A man who has friends must himself be friendly,
but there is a friend who sticks closer than a brother.

Proverbs 18:24 (NKJV)

Chapter Nine

ॐ

Marriage Spice

First, a man must choose his love, then he must love his choice.

Henry Smith

How to Prepare a Husband

From the St. Paul's Methodist Episcopal Church Cookbook, Cedar Rapids, Iowa 1915.

A good many husbands are entirely spoiled by mismanagement in cooking, so they are not tender and good. Some women keep them constantly in hot water; others freeze them. Some roast them; others put them in a stew. Still others keep them constantly in a pickle.

It is far better to have none than not to know how to pick a husband properly.

In selecting your husband you should not be guided by the silvery appearance as in buying mackerel, nor by the golden tint as in salmon. Be sure and select him yourself because tastes differ.

If he sputters or fizzes while cooking, do not be anxious—some husbands do this. Add a little sugar in the form of what confectioners call kisses, but no vinegar. A little spice improves a husband but must be used with judgment. Stir gently the while, lest he become flat and tasteless. Under no circumstances should he be poked with sharp instruments to test tenderness.

If thus treated you will find husbands become digestible and able to keep a lifetime.

Author Unknown

$\mathcal{S}$pelling Test

Once my wife asked me, "How do you spell love?"

"L-O-V-E?" I replied, spelling out the word.

"No," she said.

"What do you want, for me to spell it in Spanish?"

"No," she explained. "You spell love T-I-M-E."

Al Denison, Christian Recording Artist

Don't only marry for better or worse, marry for good.

L.E.S.

"Haven't you read," Jesus replied, "that at the beginning the Creator 'made them male and female,' and said, 'For this reason a man will leave his father and mother and be united to his wife, and the two will become one flesh'? So they are no longer two, but one. Therefore what God has joined together, let man not separate."

Matthew 19:4-6

*Q*uick and Easy Romantic Dinner for Two

Instructions:

1. Feed the children and put them to bed early.
2. Lower the lights.
3. Play soft music.
4. Order Chinese food.
5. After dinner, watch an old, romantic video.

L.E.S.

*M*y Prayer

Do I love him? Do I not?

My feelings oft are varied.

So I pray and often plot

To love the man I married.

Unknown

Chapter Ten

ও

Wholesome Children

Children have more need of models than of critics.

Folk Proverb

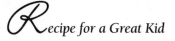

Recipe for a Great Kid

Cook's Note: *Be careful not to allow children to spoil.*

Ingredients:
One child (any variety)
1 cup affection
1 cup discipline
1 full knowledge of God
1 pint wisdom
12 cups education
1 portion fun and play

Directions:

Take one child, any shape, size, gender, or ability. Mix with affection and discipline, packed fairly, yet firmly. Stir in goodly knowledge of God (you cannot add too much of this). Fold with wisdom. Allow child to taste consequences—overprotection usually keeps him from the ability to make wise decisions. To help your child rise to full potential, mix in education and help with homework. Add one portion of each day for playing together and sharing fun (see recipe on next page).

Treasure and cherish your child with all your heart.

L.E.S.

Bubble Recipe

Cook's Note: *Here's a way to have fun with your children: create bubbles and run around chasing them—the bubbles that is!*

Directions:

Add one part mild dishwashing liquid detergent to three parts water and stir gently.

To make mounds of bubbles, pour mixture on flat surface. Place end of drinking straw into mixture and gently blow.

For bigger bubbles, twist a 12-inch piece of wire into a loop with a handle to make a bubble wand. Or, use the plastic rings that hold a six-pack of soda together.

He who laughs...lasts.

Tim Hansel, Author

*M*ake Time for Kids

Cook's Note: *In order not to see your ever-changing child slip through your fingers, use this recipe. You will enjoy it as much as your child.*

Ingredients:

You

Your child

This moment

1 book, toy, or game (optional)

1 pinch words (optional)

Directions:

Stop what you're doing and call your child's name with a happy lilt in your voice. You may add a book, a toy or a favorite game to this mix. But the most important ingredient is the moment. Accentuate the moment by serving kind words to your child, prompting him or her to serve words back to you. (You may occasionally skip the final ingredient and relish just being together.)

L.E.S.

Her children arise up, and call her blessed.

Proverbs 31:28 (KJV)

*O*n Defrosting Children

Cook's Note: *If your child is frozen in front of the television set,*
you may need to defrost him so brain damage does not occur. To determine if your child is
frozen, watch for unblinking eyes, pale skin, and monosyllabic responses.

Ingredients:
1 dozen books
1 long walk
5 toys
1/2 pd. games
1 hour homework
1 weekly trip to library
1/2 dozen crafts
1 daily story time

Directions:
To undo damage, add any combination of ingredients and stir gently.

Caution: When you assert firm pressure to turn your child's eyes from the TV, expect to encounter some form of trauma such as screaming, temper tantrums, and tears.

Do not lose your cool. Stick with your resolve. The results will be a child who is more robust, inquisitive and happy.

L.E.S.

Part Four

ઢ

Just Desserts

*A cheerful look brings joy to the heart,
and good news gives health to the bones.*

Psalm 15:30

Chapter Eleven

ॐ

Warming Forgiveness

The best way to disagree is very gently.

L.E.S.

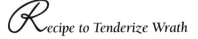

Recipe to Tenderize Wrath

Ingredients:
1 hatchet
3 drops mercy
1 full pardon

Directions:
Bury your hatchet, but not in the back of your friend's head. Put wrath in a large bowl and marinate it with 3 drops of mercy and one full pardon. Grill over low heat for well-done forgiveness.

Serve forgiveness to those who don't deserve it, just as God did for you.

L.E.S.

We should forgive and then forget what we have forgiven.

Anonymous

*H*ow to Make an Apology

Cook's Note: *This is one of the most difficult recipes, but reconciliation makes it most rewarding.*

Ingredients:
1 sincere prayer
1 poached ego
5 cups guts
3 sincere words
1 humble pie (recipe follows)

Directions:
Start with prayer asking God to help you apologize to the person you have wronged. Poach ego well and add all the guts. When you face your friend, stir in 3 sincere words: "I am sorry." Serve with humble pie.

L.E.S.

Speak ill of no man but speak all the good you know of everybody.

Benjamin Franklin, American Author and Statesman

*H*ow to Make Humble Pie

Cook's Note: *This easy pie is simply mm-mm good!*

Custard Filling Ingredients:

2 eggs

3 cups milk

1/8 teaspoon salt

4 tablespoons sugar

Sprinkle of nutmeg

Whipped cream topping

1 teaspoon vanilla

1 unbaked pie shell

Directions:

Beat eggs, then combine milk with salt, sugar and vanilla. Mix well before pouring into pie shell. Sprinkle surface of pie with nutmeg to taste. Bake in 450° oven for 10 minutes. Reduce oven temperature to 325°, bake for 40 minutes longer. Test to see if done by inserting a knife blade into center. If done, blade will be clean. Cool pie for 10 minutes before adding whipped cream topping.

Serve humbly to the person you've wronged.

Chapter Twelve

⁊&

Cooling Disappointments

I am not so concerned you have fallen but that you rise.

Abraham Lincoln, 16th United States President

*W*hen Dreams Die

Cook's Note: *Your character is what you have left when you've lost everything else. Like sweet herbs, it gives off the finest fragrance when pressed.*

Ingredients:
1 Master Chef
1 dead dream
1 character

Directions:
Press dead dream into the Master Chef's hands. Ask that he will revive your dream or give you a new one.

Let go of the dream.

Wait expectantly for the Master Chef to press your character and release its precious oils to enhance lives of others and your own.

L.E.S.

Never return borrowed trouble.

L.E.S.

$\mathcal{R}$ecipe for a Fresh Start

Cook's Note: *Sometimes, in following a recipe, certain things go wrong; your casserole is burnt or becomes too soupy or dry. Don't panic. You can always make a fresh start.*

Ingredients:

1 new beginning
2 cups expectation
2 ounces patience

Directions:

Gather ingredients from your original recipe and add new beginning by trying again. Blend expectations with patience and bake at an even temperature. Serve to your friends and family.

L.E.S.

Success may not be permanent, but neither is failure.

L.E.S.

$\mathscr{H}$ow to Make an Attitude Adjustment

Cook's Note: *This recipe is just right for shrinking a swollen ego.*

Ingredients:
1 chunk bitterness
1 gallon water
1 pound meaningful work
1 cup mirth
1 pint good manners
1 fresh perspective (optional)

Directions:
So as not to leave an aftertaste in the mouths of those to whom you serve it, soak bitterness in full gallon of fresh water for an hour; drain. Cut into bite-sized pieces and sift with meaningful work and mirth. Stir in good manners.

Bake during waking hours. If attitude shrivels during baking, stir in a fresh perspective.

L.E.S.

Chapter Thirteen

≥♠

Beating the Blues

Our hope despairs yet our despair still hopes.

Martin Luther, Theologian

*H*ow to Beat the Blues

Ingredients:
A bunch of worries
1 pound prayer
1 can thankfulness
1 package praise

Directions:

To beat the blues, you must first stop stewing: turn off burner under pot of tomorrow's worries. Turn heat down under today's pot and simmer gently for 1 minute. Stir in prayer and allow to simmer a full hour. Remove from heat. Slowly beat in thankfulness and praise at high speed until lumps disappear and mixture becomes light and frothy. Turn out and form into balls of contentment.

L.E.S.

A faith lift is a great cure for wrinkles of worry.

L.E.S.

Don't worry if your job is small and your rewards few;
remember that the mighty oak was once a nut like you.

Anonymous

*T*op Ten Ways to Win over Worry

1. Don't give up. Hope in God.
2. Walk by faith not by sight.
3. Take time out for a good laugh.
4. Use the Bible as a window to see your world.
5. Never trouble trouble until trouble troubles you.
6. Make choices based on God's word.
7. Give thanks to the LORD, for he is good.
8. Ask for God's strength to get you through.
9. Stop and enjoy the moment.
10. Pray as if everything depended upon God—it does.

L.E.S.

I consider that our present sufferings are not worth comparing with the glory that will be revealed in us.

Romans 8:18

$\mathcal{T}$hinning a Middle-Age Spread

Cook's Note: *If you've noticed Middle-Aged Spread hugging you, you may release its grip by throwing this get-together in her honor.*

Guest List:
Daily Exercise
Green Leafy Veggies
Fruit
Lean Meats
Grains

Directions:

Send an invitation to your friend, Daily Exercise. Invite her to join you and Middle-Aged Spread every day for a walk around the block or to dance to an exercise video. You might want to try turning the volume down on the video so you can listen to a cassette tape of a novel from the library.

The two of you should meet Green Leafy Veggies for lunch and invite Fruit for dessert. Share an early dinner later on with Lean Meats and Grains. Invite Veggies again. Continue this routine and Middle-Aged Spread will loosen her grip—until the holidays when she will return for a seven-pound visit. Re-introduce her to your guests no later than January 2.

L.E.S.

Part Five

❧

Garnishes of Celebrations

*"When you give a banquet, invite the poor, the crippled, the lame,
the blind, and you will be blessed."*

Luke 14:13-14

Chapter Fourteen

ॐ

Basting Birthdays

You can't help getting older, but you don't have to get old.

George Burns (Age 90), Actor and Comedian

*O*melet *for the Young at Heart*

Cook's Note: *You are only as old as you feel.*

Ingredients:

4 egg-ceptional passions
1/2 cup milk of enthusiasm
Minced disappointments
1 clove bad habits, crushed

A few fresh starts
1 can cream of age soup
Wisdom's paprika to taste

Directions:

In small mixing bowl, beat egg-ceptional passions with enthusiasm until blended lightly. Sauté disappointments with crushed bad habits over medium heat until translucent. Pour in passion/enthusiasm mixture and continue to cook until soft inside and golden outside. While omelet is cooking, heat in saucepan cream of aged soup with a few fresh starts, only until sauce warms; do not boil.

Turn omelet onto plate and cover with creamy sauce. Sprinkle with wisdom and garnish with a sprig of not-taking-yourself-too-seriously. Serve for many days to come. Enjoy to your heart's content.

L.E.S.

Never make fun of your host's coffee. You may be old and weak someday yourself.

L.E.S.

*B*irthday Blessing

Lord, allow me to have another year to marinate in the flavor of you
so I may be tender toward others. Help me appreciate the meaty blessings
you have skewered into my life. Salt me with opportunities
to serve others as you pepper my life with your will.
Grill away the fat of fear and anger as I learn to trust you more.
In your name. Amen.

L.E.S.

If wrinkles must be written upon our brows,
let them not be written upon the heart.
The spirit should not grow old.

James A. Garfield, 20th United States President

Top Ten Almost-Free Birthday Gifts For...

Children—A large empty box. With imagination it can become a car, plane, house, rocket or ship. Help decorate the box.

Caution: A child should never play in the box in the driveway.

Older Children, High Schoolers, Collegians—Nothing hits the spot like cold, hard cash, it's true. But if you want to give them something very special, give a gift of your time. Take the student to a special event, horseback riding or fishing.

Newlyweds—Dinner for two at your home. Prepare the meal, set the table, and play the part of food server. Then, make an exit and give them time alone.

Husbands—A homecooked dinner featuring his favorite dessert.

Note: Send the kids to a baby-sitter for the evening.

Friends—A tea party with china cups and pretty pastries.

Mothers—Avoid all cooking and cleaning appliances; go for fuzzy houseshoes or breakfast in bed.

Dads—Tickets to his favorite team's upcoming game or a very clean garage.

Grandmothers or Grandfathers—No trinkets, please! Try a scarf, some lotion, or a gift certificate at their favorite store. Consider giving a most favored gift: a visit from you.

L.E.S.

Recipe for a Fortieth Birthday

Cook's Note: *Most people are never ready for this, but it might get you through the day as well as the next decade.*

Ingredients:

1 box reflections	5 parts work
7 ounces of love	5 parts play
A few goals	1 red sports car (optional)
1 cup energy	

Directions:

Dip a healthy dose of reflections into your mix of life. As you savor the taste, you may be tempted to substitute the ingredient called spouse for another of a different size and shape. To avoid heartache and grief, stir an additional heapful of love with the spouse you already have. Add new goals from the vine of ideas. Avoid gaudy, glittery goals that may add a metallic taste. Count your blessings and spend your energy on finding the balance between work and play. If prepared with care, this dish of happiness should last another 40 years.

L.E.S.

Forty is the old age of youth; fifty is the youth of old age.

Folk Proverb

Chapter Fifteen

Toasting Brides

*The best way for a newlywed to clinch an argument
is to take him in her arms.*

L.E.S.

Blessing for a Bride and Groom

Lord, bless this courtship as it sails into the sea of matrimony.
To weather the storms of life, give this marriage strong riggings and safe harbors.
May the ship's sails be full of the winds of joy so they may
find passage to their fairest dreams.
Let the waves of life gently move this couple to love
one another in ever-deepening ways.
Enable them to navigate their hearts
not only to each other, but to you.

L.E.S.

$\mathcal{R}$ecipe for Building a Happy Marriage

Cook's Note: *Judging by the divorce rate a lot of people who said I do, didn't.*

Ingredients:
10 I do's
10 I don'ts

Directions:

I do:

Think about my spouse's good qualities.

Try to know my spouse on a deeper level.

Squelch selfish thoughts.

Change *myself* for the better.

Do something kind for my mate every day.

Make compromises.

Spend time with my spouse.

Forgive him/her.

Listen to him/her, making eye contact.

Hug my spouse several times a day.

I don't:

Try to change my spouse.

Try to get my own way.

Try to win every argument.

Think only of myself.

Concentrate on my spouse's bad qualities.

Ignore him/her.

Interrupt him/her.

Give him/her the silent treatment.

Try to punish my mate.

Expect my spouse to be perfect.

L.E.S.

Easy Wedding Punch

Cook's Note: *This is good stuff! We served it at my wedding and we've been married 18 years!*

Ingredients:
1 can apple juice concentrate
1 can pineapple juice concentrate
1 quart bottle chilled 7-Up™
1 can Hawaiian Punch™ concentrate, thawed
Ice

Directions:

Take apple juice and pineapple juice concentrates from the freezer 3 hours before serving. Put into punch bowl. Chip concentrate with ice pick. Stir in 7-Up™ and Hawaiian Punch™. Add ice. Serves 25.

Chapter Sixteen

ॐ

Baby Cakes

A baby is a miracle of love.

Brenda Hunter, Ph.D.

A crying baby can be a pain in the neck when he is around.
But he is a pain in the heart when he grows up and is not.

L.E.S.

Children need strength to lean on, a shoulder to cry on, and an example to learn from.

Anonymous

Baby's Blessing

Bless this child of mine,

Grant him ways to shine.

Spare him from harm's way,

Hear him when he prays.

Make me wise to guide,

This one by my side.

Let him grow to be,

Joy to you and me.

L.E.S.

To the Adopted Baby...

Not flesh of my flesh

nor bone of my bone

but miraculously my own.

Never forget—even for a minute

you weren't born under my heart

but in it.

Fleur Conkling Hejlinger, *Saturday Evening Post*, 1952

An alarm clock is a device for awakening people who don't have small children.

Anonymous

Toddlers are a lot like airplanes. You only hear him when he crashes.

L.E.S.

Give your child both roots and wings.

Unknown

Chapter Seventeen

ॐ

Saucy Dinner Parties

The best way to serve spinach is to someone else.

Anonymous

*N*eighborhood Soup

Cook's Note: *While this simmers, you will have a chance to use a chilly afternoon to catch up with neighbors.*

Invitation:

Invite your neighbors to bring vegetables of their choice, scrubbed and diced.

Ingredients:

Vegetables	1 soup bone
3-quart pan boiling water	1 pound lean beef, diced
1 cup rice	Salt to taste

Directions:

Add soup bone and beef to 3 quarts salted water. Bring to a boil; reduce heat. Add rice and simmer covered for 1 hour and 30 minutes. Add vegetables. Simmer covered for an additional 30 minutes or until tender. Serve steaming hot.

L.E.S.

Better a meal of vegetables where there is love than a fattened calf with hatred.

Proverbs 15:17

"Give us today our daily bread."

Matthew 6:11

Blessings for a Meal

God is great, God is good,

And we thank Him for our food,

By His hand we are fed;

Thank you, Lord, for our daily bread.

Author Unknown

For health and food,

For love and friends,

For everything

Thy goodness sends,

Father in Heaven,

We thank Thee.

Ralph Waldo Emerson, American Philosopher and Essayist

*H*ow to Warm Up a Hungry Crowd

Cook's Note: *This chili recipe serves a crowd on a cold day.*

Ingredients:
2 cups chopped onion

2 tablespoons oil

3 pounds ground beef

4 cups water

2 teaspoons dried parsley

3 15-ounce cans pinto beans

1 16-ounce can tomato puree

1/3 cup chili powder

1 tablespoon salt

1 teaspoon pepper

1 teaspoon cumin

1 cup cheddar cheese

Directions:
Sauté onion and ground beef in oil; drain excess fat. Combine beef and onion mixture with rest of the ingredients. Heat until bubbly. Turn down heat, cover and simmer for 45 minutes. Uncover and simmer another 30 minutes. Remove excess fat. Grate cheese and sprinkle on top. Serve with corn chips. Makes 4 quarts.

If you don't believe turnip greens are better than nothing,
ask someone who has tried both.

Unknown

Health rule: eat like a king for breakfast,
a prince for lunch, and a pauper for dinner.

Anonymous

Epilogue

Most of life revolves around your kitchen.
So be prepared to serve others and yourself. Keep your
pantry full of love and patience and you will never
run out of good company or a happy family. Preparing
these recipes takes a lot of work, but the results are
rewarding. If you watch your boiling pots and
regularly mop up any spills, you will be able to
consistently serve *Love's Little Recipes for Life!*
to the people you love.

Linda E. Shepherd

Acknowledgments

Grateful acknowledgment is made to the authors and publishers for the use of the following material. Every effort has been made to contact original sources. If notified, I will be pleased to rectify any omissions in future editions.

Selected quotes referenced as Anonymous, from *14,000 Quips & Quotes For Speakers, Writers, Editors, Preachers, and Teachers,* by E. C. McKenzie, © 1980 Baker House Book Company. Used by permission.

"Notice" and *"How to Prepare Husbands,"* from *St. Paul's Episcopal Methodist Church Cookbook,* 1915. Used by permission of St. Paul's United Methodist Church, Cedar Rapids, Iowa.

"Recipe for a Happy Home," from *Butter 'n Recipes,* Beaumont District IAPES. Used by permission.

To the Adopted Baby, Fleur Conkling Hejlinger, *Saturday Evening Post,* 1952. Used by permission.

It Couldn't be Done, Edgar A. Guest, *The Path to Home,* The Reilly and Lee Company.

Linda Shepherd can be reached via email at: Lswrites@aol.com